British Virgin Islands

Everything You Need to Know

Introduction to the British Virgin Islands 6

Geography and Climate 8

Early History: A Tale of Indigenous Inhabitants 10

Colonial Era: European Exploration and Settlement 12

The Plantation Period: Sugar, Slavery, and Trade 14

Emancipation and the Post-Colonial Era 16

Modern Development: Economy and Infrastructure 19

Government and Politics in the BVI 22

Flora and Fauna: Exploring BVI's Natural Beauty 25

Delving into BVI Cuisine: Flavors of the Islands 28

The Charter Capital: Nautical Adventures in BVI 31

Majestic Sights: Must-See Attractions in BVI 33

Road Town: Heartbeat of the British Virgin Islands 35

Spanish Town: A Glimpse into History 38

The Charm of Virgin Gorda 40

Exploring Jost Van Dyke: Tales of Pirates and Paradise 42

Anegada: The Unique Coral Island 45

Cultural Diversity in BVI: Blend of Traditions 47

Music and Dance: Vibrant Cultural Expressions 50

Festivals and Celebrations: Year-Round Merriment 53

Arts and Crafts: Creativity in the Caribbean 56

Family and Community: Social Fabric of BVI 59

Religion and Spirituality: Faith in the Islands 62

Education System in BVI: Nurturing Minds 65

4

Healthcare and Wellness: Living Well in Paradise 68

Economy and Trade: From Sugarcane to Tourism 71

Transportation Networks: Getting Around the Islands 74

Conservation Efforts: Preserving BVI's Natural Heritage 77

Hurricane Resilience: Weathering the Storms 80

British Influence: Legacy and Impact 83

American Connection: Shared Histories and Futures 86

Caribbean Identity: BVI's Place in the Region 89

Local Dialects and Languages: Communicating in BVI 92

Cultural Etiquette: Navigating Social Norms 94

Traditional Dress and Attire: Fashion in the Islands 97

Sports and Recreation: Active Lifestyles in BVI 99

Environmental Sustainability: Green Initiatives 101

Legal System and Justice: Laws of the Land 104

Tourism Industry: Driving Force of the Economy 107

Historical Landmarks and Heritage Sites 110

Indigenous People: Guardians of BVI's Past 113

Future Prospects: Vision for a Thriving BVI 115

Epilogue 117

Introduction to the British Virgin Islands

In the azure waters of the Caribbean Sea lies a cluster of paradisiacal islands known as the British Virgin Islands (BVI). These jewels of the Caribbean are a haven for travelers seeking pristine beaches, lush landscapes, and a rich tapestry of history and culture. Comprising over 60 islands and cays, the BVI boasts some of the most breathtaking scenery in the region.

Steeped in a colonial past, the British Virgin Islands have a captivating history that dates back centuries. Originally inhabited by the Arawak and Carib peoples, the islands were later discovered by European explorers, including Christopher Columbus in 1493. However, it was not until the early 17th century that the British established a permanent presence, using the islands primarily for their strategic location and fertile soil.

During the colonial era, the British Virgin Islands flourished as centers of sugarcane production, fueled by the labor of enslaved Africans. The remnants of this dark period can still be seen in the old plantation estates scattered across the islands. With the abolition of slavery in the 19th century, the BVI underwent a period of transition, eventually emerging as a self-governing territory within the British Empire. Today, the British

Virgin Islands are celebrated for their vibrant culture, warm hospitality, and stunning natural beauty. Each island offers its own unique charm, from the bustling streets of Road Town on Tortola to the secluded beaches of Anegada. Visitors flock to the BVI to indulge in world-class sailing, snorkeling, and diving, while others come to immerse themselves in the local culture and cuisine. Despite their small size, the British Virgin Islands play an outsized role in the global economy, thanks in large part to their thriving tourism industry. With a reputation for luxury and exclusivity, the BVI attract affluent travelers from around the world, drawn by the promise of secluded resorts and pristine beaches.

But beyond the sun, sea, and sand, the British Virgin Islands are also home to a diverse and resilient population, whose roots stretch back generations. From the colorful festivals and celebrations that dot the calendar to the vibrant music and dance traditions that animate daily life, the culture of the BVI is a testament to the resilience and creativity of its people.

As we embark on this journey through the British Virgin Islands, we invite you to explore the rich tapestry of history, culture, and natural beauty that defines this enchanting corner of the Caribbean. Whether you're a seasoned traveler or a first-time visitor, there's something here for everyone to discover and enjoy. So sit back, relax, and let the magic of the BVI sweep you away.

Geography and Climate

Nestled in the northeastern Caribbean Sea, the British Virgin Islands (BVI) form a picturesque archipelago of over 60 islands and cays. Situated to the east of Puerto Rico and the US Virgin Islands, the BVI is renowned for its stunning natural beauty and favorable climate.

Geographically, the islands are divided into four main groups: the Tortola Group, the Virgin Gorda Group, the Anegada Group, and the Jost Van Dyke Group. The largest and most populous island is Tortola, home to the capital, Road Town, as well as the territory's main port and commercial center. Virgin Gorda, known for its distinctive boulders and luxury resorts, is the second-largest island, followed by the coral atoll of Anegada and the rugged outpost of Jost Van Dyke.

The terrain of the British Virgin Islands varies widely, from verdant hills and valleys to rocky cliffs and white sandy beaches. Tortola boasts the highest peak in the archipelago, Mount Sage, which rises to an elevation of 1,716 feet (523 meters) and offers panoramic views of the surrounding islands. Meanwhile, the flat and low-lying landscape of Anegada stands in stark contrast to the volcanic topography of its neighbors.

Blessed with a tropical maritime climate, the British Virgin Islands enjoy warm temperatures year-round, moderated by trade winds blowing in from the northeast. Average temperatures hover around 80°F (27°C) in the winter months and climb to around 90°F (32°C) in the summer. Rainfall is heaviest between September and November, during the peak of hurricane season, while the dry season extends from December to May.

The islands are vulnerable to tropical storms and hurricanes, which can wreak havoc on the fragile ecosystem and infrastructure. However, the British Virgin Islands have developed robust disaster preparedness and mitigation measures to minimize the impact of these natural disasters. Despite the occasional threat of severe weather, the BVI remains a popular destination for travelers seeking sun, sand, and relaxation in a tropical paradise.

Early History: A Tale of Indigenous Inhabitants

Long before the arrival of European explorers, the British Virgin Islands were inhabited by indigenous peoples. These original inhabitants, primarily of Arawak and Carib descent, lived off the land and sea, forming a vibrant and complex society that thrived for centuries.

Archaeological evidence suggests that the first humans settled in the region around 1500 BCE, establishing small villages along the coastlines of the islands. These early settlers were skilled fishermen and farmers, cultivating crops such as cassava, sweet potatoes, and maize in the fertile soil of the islands. They also relied on the abundant marine resources, including fish, shellfish, and turtles, to sustain their communities.

Over time, these indigenous peoples developed sophisticated social and political structures, with chiefs or caciques ruling over extended kinship networks. They also created intricate pottery and stone tools, which served both practical and ceremonial purposes. Trade networks extended throughout the Caribbean, connecting the British Virgin Islands with neighboring islands and mainland South America.

The arrival of the Caribs, a more aggressive and warlike group, around 1000 CE, brought significant changes to the region. The Caribs, known for their seafaring prowess and warrior culture, gradually displaced or assimilated the Arawak peoples, asserting dominance over the islands. Despite occasional conflicts between rival groups, trade and cultural exchange continued to flourish, enriching the diverse tapestry of indigenous life in the Caribbean.

European contact with the indigenous peoples of the British Virgin Islands began in the late 15th century, with the arrival of Spanish explorers such as Christopher Columbus. These encounters, initially characterized by curiosity and trade, soon gave way to conflict and exploitation, as European powers vied for control of the lucrative resources of the New World. The indigenous populations were decimated by disease, warfare, and enslavement, leaving behind a legacy of loss and displacement that continues to resonate in the region today.

Despite the tragic consequences of European colonization, the indigenous peoples of the British Virgin Islands left an indelible mark on the history and culture of the region. Their descendants, though greatly diminished in number, continue to preserve and celebrate their ancestral heritage, ensuring that the legacy of the indigenous inhabitants lives on in the modern-day BVI.

Colonial Era: European Exploration and Settlement

The Colonial Era in the British Virgin Islands marks a significant chapter in its history, characterized by European exploration and settlement. It was during this period that the islands were first claimed by European powers, laying the foundations for the cultural and political landscape that exists today.

The first Europeans to set foot in the British Virgin Islands were Spanish explorers, led by Christopher Columbus, who arrived in the late 15th century. However, it wasn't until the early 17th century that the islands came under the control of the English crown. In 1612, English settlers from neighboring St. Kitts established the first permanent European settlement on the island of Tortola, marking the beginning of British colonization in the region.

The colonization of the British Virgin Islands was driven by a desire for land, resources, and strategic advantage in the Caribbean. The islands' fertile soil and favorable climate made them ideal for the cultivation of cash crops such as sugarcane, tobacco, and cotton. Plantations sprang up across the islands, worked by enslaved Africans who were forcibly brought to the region to meet the growing demand for labor.

The colonial economy of the British Virgin Islands was heavily reliant on slavery, with enslaved Africans forming the backbone of the labor force. Conditions on the plantations were harsh, and resistance to slavery was met with brutal repression. Despite these challenges, enslaved Africans found ways to resist and assert their humanity, preserving their cultural traditions and forging bonds of solidarity within their communities.

Throughout the colonial era, the British Virgin Islands were caught up in the power struggles and conflicts that defined the broader Caribbean region. The islands changed hands several times between the English, Dutch, and Spanish, as European powers jockeyed for control of the lucrative sugar trade. Despite these geopolitical upheavals, the British Virgin Islands remained under British control for much of the colonial period, eventually becoming a British crown colony in 1672.

The legacy of the colonial era is still visible in the architecture, culture, and society of the British Virgin Islands today. The islands' colonial past has left an indelible imprint on their identity, shaping everything from their language and legal system to their social and economic structures. As we explore the colonial history of the British Virgin Islands, we gain insight into the forces that have shaped the islands and their people over the centuries.

The Plantation Period: Sugar, Slavery, and Trade

The Plantation Period in the British Virgin Islands represents a pivotal era in its history, characterized by the establishment of sugar plantations, the expansion of the slave trade, and the rise of a wealthy elite class. Beginning in the 17th century and lasting well into the 19th century, this period saw the islands transformed into major centers of sugar production, fueled by the labor of enslaved Africans.

Sugar emerged as the dominant crop in the British Virgin Islands due to its high demand in Europe and the profitability of its production. Large plantations, owned by wealthy European settlers and absentee landowners, sprang up across the islands, covering vast swathes of land and employing hundreds of enslaved Africans. These plantations were meticulously organized and managed, with each stage of the sugar production process carefully orchestrated to maximize efficiency and profit. The labor-intensive nature of sugar cultivation required a large workforce, leading to the mass importation of enslaved Africans from West Africa. These enslaved Africans were subjected to brutal conditions, forced to work long hours in the fields under the harsh Caribbean sun. Many died from exhaustion, disease, or violence, while others endured unimaginable suffering in their quest for survival.

The plantation economy of the British Virgin Islands was closely tied to the transatlantic slave trade, which saw millions of Africans forcibly transported to the Americas to fuel the demand for cheap labor. British slave ships sailed from West Africa to the Caribbean, carrying human cargo destined for the plantations of the BVI and other colonies in the region. The transatlantic slave trade not only enriched European slave traders and plantation owners but also devastated African societies and cultures, leaving a lasting legacy of trauma and exploitation. Despite the brutality of slavery, enslaved Africans in the British Virgin Islands found ways to resist and assert their humanity. They formed tight-knit communities, forged bonds of kinship and solidarity, and preserved their cultural traditions through music, dance, and storytelling. Acts of rebellion and resistance were not uncommon, as enslaved Africans fought against their oppressors and sought freedom and justice. The Plantation Period in the British Virgin Islands came to an end in the mid-19th century with the abolition of slavery throughout the British Empire. The emancipation of enslaved Africans brought about profound changes to the social, economic, and political landscape of the islands, paving the way for a new era of freedom and self-determination. Yet, the legacy of the plantation period continues to shape the identity of the British Virgin Islands, reminding us of the enduring impact of slavery and the resilience of those who endured it.

Emancipation and the Post-Colonial Era

The period following emancipation in the British Virgin Islands marked a profound shift in the social, economic, and political landscape of the territory. With the abolition of slavery in 1834, thousands of formerly enslaved Africans gained their freedom, ushering in a new era of hope and possibility. However, the transition from slavery to freedom was not without its challenges, as newly freed individuals faced systemic discrimination, economic exploitation, and social marginalization.

In the immediate aftermath of emancipation, many formerly enslaved Africans struggled to secure land, employment, and basic rights. The plantation economy, which had been built on the backs of enslaved labor, underwent significant changes as former slaves sought to establish themselves as independent farmers and entrepreneurs. Some were able to acquire small plots of land through government grants or purchase, while others found work as laborers on the estates of former slaveholders.

The post-emancipation period also witnessed the emergence of new social and cultural movements, as formerly enslaved Africans sought to assert their dignity, identity, and autonomy. Churches became important centers of community life, providing spiritual guidance, education, and support to the newly freed population. Religious and cultural practices, including music, dance, and storytelling, played a crucial role in preserving and celebrating African heritage in the face of assimilation and cultural erasure.

Despite the promise of freedom, the legacy of slavery continued to cast a long shadow over the British Virgin Islands, shaping patterns of inequality and injustice for generations to come. The colonial government, dominated by wealthy landowners and merchants, maintained tight control over the political and economic life of the territory, perpetuating a system of exploitation and oppression that favored the interests of the ruling elite.

In the decades following emancipation, the British Virgin Islands experienced significant social and economic change, as the territory transitioned from a plantation-based economy to a more diversified and modern society. The growth of the tourism industry, coupled with investments in infrastructure and education, helped to fuel economic development and improve living standards for many residents. However, disparities in wealth and opportunity persisted, as marginalized communities continued to struggle for equality and justice.

The post-colonial era in the British Virgin Islands was marked by a gradual transition toward self-governance and autonomy. In 1956, the territory was granted its own constitution, providing for the establishment of a legislative council and the election of local representatives. Over the years, the British Virgin Islands have continued to assert their sovereignty and independence, while maintaining close ties to the United Kingdom as a British Overseas Territory.

Today, the British Virgin Islands stand as a testament to the resilience and spirit of its people, who have overcome centuries of adversity to build a vibrant and thriving society. As we reflect on the emancipation and post-colonial era in the BVI, we are reminded of the enduring legacy of slavery and the ongoing struggle for freedom, justice, and equality in the Caribbean and beyond.

Modern Development: Economy and Infrastructure

In the modern era, the British Virgin Islands have undergone significant development, transforming from a largely agrarian society into a thriving hub of commerce, tourism, and finance. Central to this transformation has been the growth of the territory's economy and the expansion of its infrastructure to support a diverse range of industries and activities.

One of the driving forces behind the modern development of the British Virgin Islands has been the growth of the tourism industry. Blessed with stunning natural beauty, including pristine beaches, crystal-clear waters, and lush tropical landscapes, the BVI has become a popular destination for travelers from around the world. Luxury resorts, boutique hotels, and yacht clubs dot the islands, catering to a discerning clientele seeking relaxation, adventure, and exclusivity.

In addition to tourism, the British Virgin Islands have emerged as a major player in the global financial services industry. The territory's favorable tax laws, political stability, and well-established legal system have made it an attractive destination for offshore banking, company incorporation, and asset management. The financial services sector contributes significantly to the territory's economy, generating revenue and creating jobs for local residents.

The growth of the economy has been accompanied by investments in infrastructure, including transportation, telecommunications, and utilities. Roads, bridges, and ports have been upgraded to facilitate the movement of goods and people throughout the islands, while telecommunications networks have been expanded to provide reliable connectivity to residents and businesses. Access to essential services such as electricity, water, and sanitation has also improved, enhancing the quality of life for residents across the territory.

Despite these advancements, the modern development of the British Virgin Islands has not been without its challenges. Rapid population growth, urbanization, and environmental degradation have placed strains on the territory's infrastructure and natural resources. Efforts to balance economic development with environmental sustainability have become increasingly important, as policymakers seek to protect the islands' fragile ecosystems while promoting continued growth and prosperity.

In recent years, the British Virgin Islands have faced additional challenges, including the impact of natural disasters such as hurricanes and the global economic downturn. These events have underscored the vulnerability of the territory's economy and infrastructure, highlighting the need for resilience and adaptation in the face of uncertainty.

As the British Virgin Islands continue to evolve and grow in the 21st century, the territory's leaders and residents remain committed to building a prosperous and sustainable future for all. By investing in infrastructure, fostering innovation, and promoting responsible stewardship of the islands' natural resources, the BVI is poised to remain a vibrant and dynamic destination for years to come.

Government and Politics in the BVI

Government and politics in the British Virgin Islands (BVI) are shaped by a unique blend of historical legacies, contemporary influences, and local aspirations. As a British Overseas Territory, the BVI maintains close ties to the United Kingdom while also enjoying a significant degree of autonomy in its internal affairs. The territory operates under a parliamentary system of government, with a constitutional monarchy headed by a governor appointed by the British monarch. The governor serves as the representative of the Crown and is responsible for overseeing the administration of the BVI, including the implementation of laws and policies.

At the local level, the British Virgin Islands are governed by a unicameral legislature known as the House of Assembly. The House of Assembly consists of 13 elected members, who are chosen by popular vote in general elections held every four years. In addition to the elected members, the legislature also includes the attorney general and two ex officio members appointed by the governor.

The premier of the British Virgin Islands is the head of government and is appointed by the governor from among the members of the House of Assembly. The premier leads the executive branch of the government and is responsible for setting policy, managing the administration, and representing the territory both domestically and internationally. The premier works closely with the cabinet, which is comprised of ministers appointed from among the elected members of the House of Assembly.

The British Virgin Islands operates under a system of parliamentary democracy, with regular elections held to determine the composition of the House of Assembly and the leadership of the government. Political parties play a central role in the electoral process, with candidates typically aligned with either the ruling party or the opposition. Campaigns are often spirited affairs, with candidates and parties vying for the support of voters through rallies, debates, and media outreach.

In recent years, government and politics in the British Virgin Islands have been shaped by a number of key issues and challenges, including economic development, environmental sustainability, and good governance. The territory has sought to diversify its economy beyond tourism and financial services, investing in sectors such as renewable energy, technology, and sustainable agriculture. Efforts to promote transparency, accountability, and public participation in decision-making have also been a focus of government reform initiatives.

Despite these efforts, the British Virgin Islands faces ongoing challenges in its political system, including concerns about corruption, inequality, and the concentration of power. Civil society organizations and advocacy groups play an important role in promoting democratic values and holding government officials accountable for their actions. As the BVI continues to navigate the complexities of modern governance, the territory remains committed to upholding the principles of democracy, rule of law, and respect for human rights.

Flora and Fauna: Exploring BVI's Natural Beauty

Exploring the flora and fauna of the British Virgin Islands unveils a stunning array of natural beauty and biodiversity. These islands, nestled in the heart of the Caribbean, are home to a rich tapestry of plant and animal life, shaped by their unique geographical location, climate, and ecosystem dynamics.

The lush landscapes of the British Virgin Islands are characterized by a diverse range of plant species, from towering mahogany trees to delicate orchids. The islands' tropical climate, with its warm temperatures and abundant rainfall, provides ideal conditions for plant growth and proliferation. Coastal mangrove forests fringe the shorelines, providing important habitat for a variety of marine species and serving as a natural buffer against erosion and storm damage.

Inland, dense rainforests carpet the hillsides, teeming with life and color. Palms, ferns, and bromeliads thrive in the humid, sheltered environment, while towering hardwoods such as the kapok and silk cotton trees provide valuable timber and shade. The islands are also home to a number of endemic plant species found nowhere else in the world, including the Virgin Islands dwarf sago palm and the Anegada ground orchid.

Beneath the waves, the waters surrounding the British Virgin Islands teem with marine life, from colorful coral reefs to majestic sea turtles. Coral reefs are among the most biodiverse ecosystems on the planet, supporting thousands of species of fish, invertebrates, and other marine organisms. The BVI's coral reefs are renowned for their beauty and diversity, attracting snorkelers, divers, and marine enthusiasts from around the world.

In addition to coral reefs, the waters of the British Virgin Islands are home to a variety of other marine habitats, including seagrass beds, mangrove swamps, and rocky shores. These habitats provide essential breeding, feeding, and nursery grounds for a wide range of marine species, including fish, crustaceans, and mollusks. Hawksbill and green sea turtles are among the most iconic residents of the BVI's waters, nesting on the islands' beaches and foraging in the surrounding seas.

The British Virgin Islands are also an important stopover and breeding ground for migratory birds, with hundreds of species passing through the islands each year. Wetlands, salt ponds, and coastal marshes provide important habitat for waterfowl, wading birds, and shorebirds, including flamingos, herons, and egrets. Birdwatchers flock to the BVI to catch a glimpse of these avian visitors, as well as to enjoy the islands' stunning natural scenery and tranquility.

As we explore the flora and fauna of the British Virgin Islands, we gain a deeper appreciation for the intricate web of life that sustains these beautiful islands. From the smallest insect to the largest whale, every creature plays a vital role in maintaining the delicate balance of nature in this tropical paradise. Through conservation efforts and responsible stewardship, we can ensure that future generations will continue to enjoy the wonders of the BVI's natural world.

Delving into BVI Cuisine: Flavors of the Islands

Delving into the cuisine of the British Virgin Islands offers a tantalizing journey through a rich tapestry of flavors, influenced by the territory's diverse cultural heritage and abundant natural resources. The culinary traditions of the BVI reflect a blend of African, European, and Caribbean influences, resulting in a vibrant and eclectic culinary landscape.

Seafood plays a central role in BVI cuisine, with fresh fish, shellfish, and crustaceans abundant in the surrounding waters. Local favorites include snapper, mahi-mahi, and lobster, often grilled, fried, or stewed and served with a variety of flavorful sauces and seasonings. Conch, a type of mollusk, is a popular ingredient in traditional dishes such as conch fritters and conch salad, prized for its tender texture and sweet, briny flavor.

In addition to seafood, BVI cuisine features a wide variety of fruits, vegetables, and spices, sourced from the islands' fertile soil and tropical climate. Plantains, yams, and cassava are staples of the BVI diet, often served as side dishes or incorporated into hearty stews and soups. Fresh fruits such as mangoes, papayas, and guavas are enjoyed year-round, either on their own or as ingredients in desserts, drinks, and savory dishes.

One of the most iconic dishes of BVI cuisine is the "roti," a type of flatbread stuffed with savory fillings such as curried meat, vegetables, or seafood. Roti is a popular street food and can be found at roadside stalls, beach bars, and local eateries throughout the islands. Another beloved dish is "fungi," a cornmeal-based side dish similar to polenta, served alongside meat, fish, or vegetables.

BVI cuisine also reflects the territory's history of plantation agriculture, with dishes such as "peas and rice" and "saltfish" serving as reminders of the islands' colonial past. Peas and rice, made with pigeon peas and rice cooked in coconut milk, is a hearty and comforting dish often served alongside grilled meat or seafood. Saltfish, a preserved form of cod or other white fish, is a staple ingredient in many BVI dishes, including breakfast favorites like "saltfish and Johnny cake."

No exploration of BVI cuisine would be complete without sampling the territory's signature beverages. Rum, distilled from sugar cane, is the spirit of choice in the BVI, with local distilleries producing a variety of high-quality rums that are enjoyed both neat and in cocktails.

"Painkiller," a tropical cocktail made with rum, pineapple juice, orange juice, and coconut cream, is a favorite among locals and visitors alike, providing a refreshing and indulgent taste of island life.

As we delve into the flavors of BVI cuisine, we discover a rich and diverse culinary heritage that reflects the territory's cultural diversity, natural abundance, and spirit of hospitality. From savory seafood dishes to tropical cocktails, every bite and sip tells a story of tradition, innovation, and the shared joy of food and fellowship in this Caribbean paradise.

The Charter Capital: Nautical Adventures in BVI

The British Virgin Islands, often dubbed the "Charter Capital of the Caribbean," offer a nautical paradise for adventurers seeking the ultimate sailing experience. With its warm, clear waters, steady trade winds, and countless coves, bays, and islands to explore, the BVI has long been a favorite destination for sailors from around the world.

The BVI's reputation as a premier sailing destination is due in large part to its ideal sailing conditions. The steady trade winds, blowing from the northeast for much of the year, provide perfect conditions for sailing, with gentle breezes and calm seas. The protected waters of the Sir Francis Drake Channel offer shelter from the open ocean, creating a safe and enjoyable environment for sailors of all skill levels. For those looking to embark on a sailing adventure in the BVI, chartering a boat is the most popular option. A wide range of charter companies offer sailboats, catamarans, and powerboats for rent, allowing visitors to explore the islands at their own pace. Many charter companies also provide experienced captains and crew, ensuring a stress-free and enjoyable sailing experience for guests. One of the highlights of sailing in the BVI is the opportunity to explore the islands' many secluded anchorages and pristine beaches. From the white sands of White Bay on Jost Van Dyke to the turquoise waters of The Baths on Virgin Gorda, each island offers its own unique charm and natural beauty. Snorkeling, diving, and swimming are popular activities, allowing sailors to discover the vibrant underwater world of coral reefs, tropical fish, and marine life. The BVI is also famous for its lively beach bars and waterfront restaurants, where sailors can relax and unwind after a day on the water. Sip on a famous Painkiller cocktail at the Soggy Dollar Bar, enjoy a delicious seafood dinner at Foxy's on Jost Van Dyke, or dance the night away at the Willy T floating bar and restaurant. The vibrant atmosphere and warm hospitality of these establishments make them a favorite destination for sailors and travelers alike. In addition to its natural beauty and vibrant culture, the BVI also offers a variety of sailing events and regattas throughout the year. The BVI Spring Regatta and Sailing Festival, held annually in March, attracts sailors from around the world to compete in a series of races and social events. Other popular events include the Leverick Bay Poker Run, the BVI Kite Jam, and the Scrub Island Invitational. Whether you're an experienced sailor or a first-time charterer, the British Virgin Islands offer an unforgettable nautical adventure that's sure to leave you with memories to last a lifetime. So hoist the sails, chart your course, and set sail for the charter capital of the Caribbean. The BVI awaits, ready to welcome you with open arms and endless possibilities for exploration and adventure on the high seas.

Majestic Sights: Must-See Attractions in BVI

When it comes to majestic sights, the British Virgin Islands (BVI) boast an impressive array of natural wonders and cultural attractions that captivate visitors from around the globe. From breathtaking beaches and lush landscapes to historic landmarks and vibrant towns, the BVI offers something for everyone to explore and enjoy.

One of the most iconic attractions in the BVI is The Baths on Virgin Gorda, a stunning geological formation featuring giant granite boulders scattered along the coastline. Visitors can wander through a maze of tunnels and grottoes, swim in crystal-clear pools, and relax on powdery white sands, surrounded by the natural beauty of this unique landscape.

Another must-see sight in the BVI is the island of Anegada, a flat coral atoll known for its pristine beaches, thriving marine life, and laid-back atmosphere. Anegada's Horseshoe Reef is the largest barrier reef in the Caribbean, offering world-class snorkeling and diving opportunities for adventurous travelers. Don't miss the chance to feast on fresh lobster at one of the island's beachfront restaurants, where you can savor the flavors of this delicious local delicacy.

For history buffs, the ruins of the Copper Mine on Virgin Gorda offer a fascinating glimpse into the island's past as a center of copper mining during the 19th century. Explore the remnants of old mine shafts, tunnels, and processing facilities, and learn about the island's rich mining heritage through interpretive signage and guided tours.

No visit to the BVI would be complete without a stop at the capital city of Road Town on Tortola, a bustling hub of culture, commerce, and Caribbean charm. Explore historic landmarks such as the Old Government House Museum and the 1780 Lower Estate Sugar Works Museum, or stroll through the colorful markets and shops lining Main Street. Be sure to sample some local cuisine at one of Road Town's many restaurants and cafes, where you can taste traditional dishes such as "roti" and "fungi" while soaking in the vibrant atmosphere of this vibrant city.

Other must-see attractions in the BVI include the scenic overlook at Sage Mountain National Park, the picturesque harbor at Soper's Hole on Tortola's West End, and the idyllic beach at White Bay on Jost Van Dyke. Whether you're seeking adventure, relaxation, or cultural immersion, the British Virgin Islands offer an abundance of majestic sights just waiting to be discovered. So pack your bags, grab your camera, and prepare to be amazed by the beauty and wonder of this Caribbean paradise.

Road Town: Heartbeat of the British Virgin Islands

Nestled on the southern coast of Tortola, Road Town stands as the bustling capital and beating heart of the British Virgin Islands (BVI). This vibrant town serves as the main hub of commerce, culture, and government in the territory, attracting visitors and residents alike with its colorful streets, historic landmarks, and lively atmosphere.

At the heart of Road Town lies Main Street, a bustling thoroughfare lined with shops, restaurants, and colonial-era buildings. Here, visitors can stroll along the waterfront, admire the colorful architecture, and soak in the sights and sounds of this bustling Caribbean town. Main Street is also home to the Crafts Alive Village, a vibrant market where local artisans showcase their handmade crafts, jewelry, and artwork.

History enthusiasts will find plenty to explore in Road Town, with a number of historic landmarks and museums scattered throughout the town. The Old Government House Museum, located on Main Street, offers insight into the territory's colonial past, with exhibits on the history of the BVI and its ties to the British monarchy. Nearby, the 1780 Lower Estate Sugar

Works Museum provides a glimpse into the island's sugar plantation era, with displays on the production of sugar, rum, and molasses.

For those interested in the arts, Road Town boasts a thriving cultural scene, with galleries, theaters, and performance spaces showcasing local talent and creativity. The BVI Art Reef, an underwater art installation located off the coast of Road Town, features sculptures and installations created by local and international artists, providing a unique opportunity for divers and snorkelers to explore the intersection of art and marine conservation.

Food lovers will delight in the culinary offerings of Road Town, with a wide range of restaurants, cafes, and eateries serving up delicious cuisine from around the world. Whether you're craving fresh seafood, Caribbean specialties, or international fare, you'll find plenty of options to satisfy your appetite in this bustling town. Don't miss the chance to sample some local favorites such as "roti," "saltfish," and "Johnny cake" at one of Road Town's many authentic eateries.

As the administrative center of the BVI, Road Town is also home to important government institutions and services, including the House of Assembly, the Supreme Court, and the Governor's Residence. The town's central location and strategic importance make it a key hub for business, transportation, and communication in the territory, with ferry terminals, marinas, and airports providing vital connections to neighboring islands and the mainland.

But perhaps the true heartbeat of Road Town lies in its people, who embody the spirit of resilience, diversity, and hospitality that defines the British Virgin Islands. Whether you're exploring historic landmarks, enjoying a meal at a local restaurant, or simply soaking in the vibrant atmosphere of Main Street, you'll find that Road Town is more than just a town—it's a vibrant and dynamic community that welcomes visitors with open arms and endless opportunities for exploration and discovery.

Spanish Town: A Glimpse into History

Nestled on the southern coast of Virgin Gorda, Spanish Town offers visitors a captivating glimpse into the history and heritage of the British Virgin Islands. Originally settled by the Spanish in the early 16th century, the town served as a strategic outpost and trading center during the colonial era. Today, Spanish Town retains much of its historic charm, with quaint streets, colonial-era buildings, and remnants of its Spanish past still visible throughout the town.

One of the most iconic landmarks in Spanish Town is the ruins of the Little Fort National Park, a 17th-century Spanish fortification perched on a hill overlooking the town and surrounding coastline. Built to defend against pirate attacks and rival European powers, the fort offers stunning panoramic views of the Sir Francis Drake Channel and neighboring islands, providing a glimpse into the town's military history and strategic importance.

Another notable attraction in Spanish Town is the Copper Mine National Park, home to the ruins of an old copper mine dating back to the 19th century. The mine was once a major source of wealth and economic activity for the island, attracting miners from around the Caribbean and beyond. Today, visitors can explore the remnants of old mine shafts, tunnels, and processing facilities, and learn about the island's rich mining heritage through interpretive signage and guided tours. Spanish Town is also home to the Virgin Gorda Yacht Harbour, a modern marina and waterfront complex that serves as a hub for boating, dining, and shopping on the island. The marina offers a range of amenities for sailors and boaters, including boat rentals, fueling stations, and yacht services, as well as waterfront restaurants, shops, and cafes where visitors can relax and enjoy the scenic views of the harbor.

In addition to its historic and cultural attractions, Spanish Town boasts some of the most beautiful beaches in the British Virgin Islands, including the famous Baths. Located just south of the town, the Baths are a geological wonderland of giant granite boulders, hidden caves, and secret pools, where visitors can explore and swim in the crystal-clear waters of the Caribbean Sea. The Baths are a popular destination for snorkeling, diving, and beachcombing, offering endless opportunities for adventure and relaxation.

As you wander the streets of Spanish Town, you'll find yourself transported back in time to an era of exploration, conquest, and adventure. From its Spanish roots to its colonial past, this charming town offers a fascinating glimpse into the history and heritage of the British Virgin Islands, inviting visitors to uncover its secrets and discover its beauty at every turn.

The Charm of Virgin Gorda

Virgin Gorda, the third-largest island in the British Virgin Islands, exudes an irresistible charm that captivates visitors with its natural beauty, serene atmosphere, and laid-back vibe. Named by Christopher Columbus for its resemblance to a reclining woman, Virgin Gorda is renowned for its stunning beaches, dramatic landscapes, and rich cultural heritage.

One of the most iconic attractions on Virgin Gorda is The Baths, a geological wonderland of giant granite boulders, hidden caves, and secret pools located on the island's southwestern coast. Visitors can explore this unique landscape by winding through narrow passages, climbing over boulders, and swimming in crystal-clear pools, surrounded by the natural beauty of the Caribbean Sea.

Virgin Gorda is also home to some of the most beautiful beaches in the British Virgin Islands, including Savannah Bay, Mahoe Bay, and Spring Bay. These pristine stretches of sand offer ideal conditions for swimming, snorkeling, and sunbathing, with calm waters, soft sands, and stunning views of the surrounding islands.

For history enthusiasts, Virgin Gorda offers a glimpse into the island's rich cultural heritage through its historic landmarks and cultural sites. The ruins of the Copper Mine, an old copper mining operation dating back to the 19th century, provide insight into the island's economic history and the legacy of colonialism in the Caribbean.

Another must-see attraction on Virgin Gorda is Gorda Peak National Park, home to the highest point on the island and a network of hiking trails that wind through lush forests and scenic vistas. At the summit, hikers are rewarded with panoramic views of the surrounding islands and the sparkling waters of the Caribbean Sea, making it the perfect spot for a picnic or a photo opportunity.

In addition to its natural beauty and historic landmarks, Virgin Gorda boasts a vibrant cultural scene, with art galleries, music festivals, and cultural events held throughout the year. Visitors can explore the island's artistic heritage through exhibitions and performances by local artists and musicians, or immerse themselves in the vibrant culture of the BVI through traditional dances, music, and cuisine.

Whether you're seeking adventure, relaxation, or cultural immersion, Virgin Gorda offers something for everyone to enjoy. From its stunning beaches and dramatic landscapes to its rich history and vibrant culture, this charming island invites visitors to discover its beauty and charm at every turn, leaving them with memories to last a lifetime.

Exploring Jost Van Dyke: Tales of Pirates and Paradise

Exploring Jost Van Dyke invites travelers to step into a world of tales intertwining pirates and paradise, where the past merges with the present amidst stunning natural beauty. This small island, part of the British Virgin Islands, has a rich history steeped in lore and legend, making it a captivating destination for adventurers and history enthusiasts alike.

Legend has it that Jost Van Dyke was named after a Dutch pirate who used the island as a hideout in the early 17th century. The island's rugged coastline, hidden coves, and secluded anchorages made it an ideal base for pirates seeking refuge from the law and a place to repair their ships. Today, visitors can explore the ruins of old pirate hideouts and imagine the swashbuckling adventures that once took place on these shores.

One of the most famous landmarks on Jost Van Dyke is the Bubbly Pool, a natural tidal pool located on the island's northeastern coast. Fed by waves crashing against the rocky shoreline, the Bubbly Pool creates a swirling whirlpool effect that delights visitors and provides a refreshing escape from the heat. The pool is accessible via a short hike through lush vegetation, offering stunning views of the surrounding coastline along the way.

Jost Van Dyke is also known for its vibrant beach bar scene, with legendary establishments such as Foxy's Tamarind Bar and Soggy Dollar Bar drawing visitors from around the world. These lively beach bars are famous for their laid-back atmosphere, live music, and potent cocktails, creating a party atmosphere that lasts long into the night. Whether you're sipping a famous Painkiller cocktail at the Soggy Dollar Bar or dancing to the sounds of reggae music at Foxy's, you're sure to have a memorable experience on Jost Van Dyke.

For those seeking a more tranquil experience, Jost Van Dyke offers plenty of opportunities to relax and unwind amidst its natural beauty. White Bay, with its powdery white sands and calm turquoise waters, is the perfect spot for swimming, sunbathing, and beachcombing. Nearby, Great Harbour offers a quieter alternative, with charming beachfront cottages, boutique shops, and local eateries serving up delicious Caribbean cuisine.

History buffs will also find plenty to explore on Jost Van Dyke, with historic landmarks such as the ruins of the Sugar Mill Plantation offering insight into the island's colonial past. Built in the

18th century, the plantation was once a thriving center of sugar production, with slaves working the fields and processing the cane into sugar and rum. Today, visitors can wander through the ruins and learn about the island's history through interpretive signage and guided tours.

As you explore Jost Van Dyke, you'll discover a place where history and legend come alive amidst stunning natural beauty, inviting you to embark on your own adventure in this Caribbean paradise. Whether you're hiking to hidden waterfalls, snorkeling in crystal-clear waters, or sipping cocktails on the beach, Jost Van Dyke offers a taste of paradise that will leave you enchanted and inspired.

Anegada: The Unique Coral Island

Anegada, the unique coral island of the British Virgin Islands, stands out among its volcanic neighbors with its flat terrain, pristine beaches, and vibrant marine life. Unlike the other islands in the BVI, which are of volcanic origin, Anegada is a low-lying coral atoll, formed by the accumulation of coral reefs and sand over millions of years.

One of the most distinctive features of Anegada is its flatness, earning it the nickname "The Drowned Island." With its highest point reaching just 28 feet above sea level, Anegada offers a stark contrast to the rugged hills and mountains of the other islands in the BVI. This unique geography has shaped the island's ecosystem, creating a haven for a variety of plant and animal species found nowhere else in the territory.

Anegada is also famous for its stunning beaches, which stretch for miles along the island's coastline. Loblolly Bay, Cow Wreck Beach, and Flash of Beauty are just a few of the pristine beaches that lure visitors with their powdery white sands, crystal-clear waters, and tranquil atmosphere. These secluded stretches of shoreline offer the perfect setting for swimming, snorkeling, sunbathing, and beachcombing, away from the crowds and commercialization found on other islands.

But perhaps the most iconic attraction on Anegada is its thriving marine ecosystem, which is home to some of the most diverse and abundant coral reefs in the Caribbean. The Horseshoe Reef, located just offshore, is the third-largest barrier reef in the world, stretching for over 18 miles and teeming with colorful coral formations, tropical fish, and other marine creatures. Snorkelers and divers flock to Anegada to explore this underwater wonderland, where they can encounter sea turtles, rays, reef sharks, and a kaleidoscope of reef fish.

In addition to its natural beauty, Anegada is also known for its delicious cuisine, with fresh seafood being a highlight of the island's culinary scene. Anegada lobster is a local delicacy and a must-try for visitors, served up in a variety of delicious dishes at beachside restaurants and eateries. Other seafood specialties include conch fritters, grilled fish, and lobster pizza, all made with the freshest ingredients sourced from the waters surrounding the island.

As you explore Anegada, you'll discover a place of unparalleled beauty and tranquility, where the rhythms of nature and the traditions of island life converge to create a truly unforgettable experience. Whether you're snorkeling in pristine waters, lounging on deserted beaches, or savoring the flavors of local cuisine, Anegada offers a glimpse into a world untouched by time, where the beauty of nature takes center stage and the spirit of adventure is alive and well.

Cultural Diversity in BVI: Blend of Traditions

The British Virgin Islands (BVI) are a vibrant tapestry of cultural diversity, shaped by centuries of migration, trade, and colonization. This archipelago in the Caribbean Sea is home to a melting pot of traditions, languages, and customs, reflecting the rich and complex history of the region.

At the heart of BVI's cultural diversity is its people, who trace their roots to Africa, Europe, Asia, and the indigenous peoples of the Caribbean. The ancestors of the Afro-Caribbean population were brought to the islands as slaves during the colonial era, contributing their languages, religions, and cultural practices to the fabric of BVI society. Today, Afro-Caribbean traditions are still celebrated and preserved through music, dance, and festivals such as the BVI Emancipation Festival, which commemorates the abolition of slavery in the territory.

In addition to Afro-Caribbean influences, the BVI is also shaped by its European heritage, particularly from the British and Dutch colonial periods. British colonial rule has left a lasting imprint on the islands, evident in the architecture, language, and legal system of the territory. English is the official language of the BVI, but you'll also hear a blend of Caribbean dialects and accents spoken by locals, reflecting the multicultural nature of the population.

The Dutch influence on the BVI is most evident on the island of Anegada, which was settled by Dutch colonists in the early 19th century. Today, Anegada retains some Dutch cultural traditions, including its unique architecture and culinary customs. Visitors to the island can sample Dutch-inspired dishes such as "souse," a traditional stew made with pickled meat, and "keshi yena," a savory cheese dish popular in Dutch Caribbean cuisine.

Asian influences are also present in BVI culture, thanks to the migration of laborers from countries such as India and China during the 19th and early 20th centuries. Indian indentured laborers brought with them their culinary traditions, including the use of spices such as curry, cumin, and turmeric in dishes such as roti, curry chicken, and dal. Chinese immigrants, meanwhile, introduced their culinary techniques and ingredients, contributing to the island's diverse food scene.

The indigenous peoples of the Caribbean also play a significant role in BVI culture, with their customs and traditions preserved through oral history, art, and archaeological sites. Petroglyphs, rock carvings, and pottery shards found throughout the islands offer glimpses into the lives and beliefs of the indigenous inhabitants who lived here long before the arrival of Europeans.

As you explore the British Virgin Islands, you'll discover a rich tapestry of cultural diversity that celebrates the unique heritage and traditions of its people. From the rhythms of Afro-Caribbean music to the flavors of Indian curry, each aspect of BVI culture tells a story of resilience, adaptation, and the enduring spirit of unity in diversity.

Music and Dance: Vibrant Cultural Expressions

In the British Virgin Islands, music and dance serve as vibrant expressions of the territory's rich cultural heritage, reflecting the diverse influences that have shaped its identity over the centuries. From the pulsating rhythms of reggae and soca to the lively movements of traditional dances, BVI's music and dance traditions are deeply ingrained in the fabric of daily life and community celebrations.

One of the most iconic music genres in the BVI is reggae, with its roots tracing back to Jamaica and the broader Caribbean. Reggae music, characterized by its infectious beats, soulful melodies, and socially conscious lyrics, has become a beloved part of BVI's musical landscape, providing a soundtrack for everything from beach parties to political rallies. Artists such as Bob Marley, Peter Tosh, and Burning Spear have left an indelible mark on BVI's reggae scene, inspiring local musicians and performers to create their own unique interpretations of the genre.

In addition to reggae, soca music also holds a prominent place in BVI's musical repertoire. Originating from Trinidad and Tobago, soca music is known for its energetic tempo, catchy hooks, and festive vibes, making it a favorite choice for carnival celebrations and dance parties. During the annual BVI Emancipation Festival, soca music fills the air as revelers take to the streets to dance, sing, and celebrate the emancipation of slaves in the territory.

Traditional music and dance are also cherished forms of cultural expression in the BVI, with roots dating back to the African diaspora and indigenous Caribbean peoples. Quadrille, a lively dance accompanied by fiddle and accordion music, is a popular folk tradition that has been passed down through generations in the BVI. Quadrille dances are often performed at weddings, festivals, and other social gatherings, with dancers moving in intricate patterns and formations to the sounds of live music.

Another traditional dance form in the BVI is the "jig," a fast-paced dance characterized by rapid footwork and lively music. Jig dancing was brought to the islands by European settlers and has since evolved into a beloved cultural tradition, with local dance troupes performing at events and festivals throughout the territory.

In recent years, the BVI has seen a resurgence of interest in traditional music and dance, with efforts underway to preserve and promote these cultural traditions for future generations.

Community organizations, schools, and cultural institutions offer classes, workshops, and performances to engage young people and instill a sense of pride in BVI's rich cultural heritage.

As you explore the British Virgin Islands, you'll encounter a vibrant tapestry of music and dance that reflects the territory's diverse cultural influences and dynamic spirit. Whether you're dancing to the rhythms of reggae at a beach bar or learning the steps of a traditional quadrille, BVI's music and dance traditions invite you to celebrate life, community, and the joy of cultural expression.

Festivals and Celebrations: Year-Round Merriment

In the British Virgin Islands, festivals and celebrations are a vibrant reflection of the territory's rich cultural heritage and diverse community spirit. Throughout the year, locals and visitors alike come together to mark special occasions, honor traditions, and celebrate life in true Caribbean style.

One of the most anticipated events in the BVI is the Emancipation Festival, held annually in late July and early August to commemorate the abolition of slavery in the territory. This multi-day festival features a colorful lineup of events, including parades, concerts, cultural performances, and street fairs. Highlights of the festival include the Miss BVI Pageant, the Calypso Competition, and the J'ouvert Morning Parade, where revelers dance through the streets in elaborate costumes to the pulsating rhythms of soca music.

Another popular festival in the BVI is the BVI Music Festival, an annual event that showcases the best of Caribbean and international music talent. Held in November, the festival features live performances by renowned artists and bands, as well as local musicians and performers. Visitors can enjoy a diverse lineup of musical genres, including reggae, soca, calypso, hip-hop, and R&B, against the backdrop of stunning beachside venues.

For food lovers, the BVI Food Fete offers a culinary celebration like no other, with a month-long series of events highlighting the diverse flavors and cuisines of the Caribbean. From gourmet food tastings and cooking demonstrations to beach barbecues and street food festivals, the BVI Food Fete showcases the best of local and international cuisine, with a focus on fresh seafood, tropical fruits, and traditional dishes.

Cultural celebrations are also an integral part of life in the BVI, with events such as the Virgin Gorda Easter Festival, the Anegada Lobster Festival, and the Tortola August Monday Parade drawing crowds from across the islands and beyond. These festivals feature traditional music, dance, and food, as well as colorful parades, competitions, and other cultural activities that celebrate the unique heritage and traditions of each island.

In addition to annual festivals, the BVI also hosts a variety of special events and celebrations throughout the year, including boat races, regattas, and religious holidays. The BVI Spring Regatta & Sailing Festival, for example, is one of the premier sailing events in the Caribbean, attracting sailors from around the world to compete in a series of races and social events. Religious holidays such as Christmas, Easter, and Carnival are also celebrated with enthusiasm and joy, with church services, feasts, and festive gatherings bringing communities together in the spirit of faith and fellowship.

As you explore the British Virgin Islands, you'll discover a calendar filled with year-round merriment and celebration, where every day offers a new opportunity to experience the warmth, hospitality, and cultural richness of this Caribbean paradise. Whether you're dancing in the streets during the Emancipation Festival, savoring the flavors of local cuisine at the BVI Food Fete, or cheering on sailors at the BVI Spring Regatta, you'll find that life in the BVI is a celebration worth savoring.

Arts and Crafts: Creativity in the Caribbean

In the British Virgin Islands, arts and crafts are a vibrant expression of the territory's cultural identity, showcasing the creativity, craftsmanship, and ingenuity of its people. From traditional handicrafts and folk art to contemporary works of sculpture and painting, BVI's arts scene is as diverse and dynamic as the islands themselves.

One of the most iconic forms of BVI's traditional arts and crafts is basket weaving, a skill passed down through generations of indigenous and Afro-Caribbean women. Using natural materials such as palm fronds, banana leaves, and sisal fibers, artisans create intricately woven baskets, hats, and bags that are both functional and decorative. These traditional crafts can be found at local markets, artisan shops, and cultural events throughout the islands, offering visitors a glimpse into the rich heritage and craftsmanship of BVI's artisans.

In addition to basket weaving, woodcarving is another cherished tradition in the BVI, with artisans creating a wide range of intricate sculptures, figurines, and decorative objects from locally sourced woods such as mahogany, cedar, and lignum vitae. These handcrafted works of art often depict scenes from BVI's natural environment, including marine life, wildlife, and landscapes, as well as cultural motifs and symbols.

Contemporary artists in the BVI are also making waves in the local and international art scene, with a growing number of galleries, studios, and exhibitions showcasing their talent and creativity. From paintings and sculptures to mixed media and digital art, BVI's contemporary artists draw inspiration from the islands' natural beauty, cultural heritage, and social issues, creating thought-provoking works that reflect the complexities of Caribbean life.

One of the most well-known contemporary artists from the BVI is Aragorn Dick-Read, whose vibrant paintings capture the spirit and essence of Caribbean life with bold colors, expressive brushwork, and dynamic compositions. His work has been exhibited in galleries and museums around the world, bringing recognition and acclaim to BVI's burgeoning art scene.

In addition to visual arts, music and dance also play a central role in BVI's cultural expression, with local musicians, dancers, and performers entertaining audiences with traditional and contemporary performances at festivals, events, and venues throughout the islands. Whether it's the rhythmic beats of steel pan music, the energetic movements of quadrille dancers, or the soulful sounds of reggae and soca, BVI's performing arts scene offers a captivating glimpse into the territory's vibrant cultural tapestry.

As you explore the British Virgin Islands, you'll discover a world of creativity and inspiration, where the arts serve as a powerful means of cultural expression, community engagement, and storytelling. Whether you're admiring the skillful craftsmanship of a woven basket, marveling at the beauty of a woodcarving, or losing yourself in the colors and textures of a contemporary painting, you'll find that BVI's arts and crafts scene is as diverse and dynamic as the islands themselves, inviting you to immerse yourself in the beauty and creativity of Caribbean culture.

Family and Community: Social Fabric of BVI

In the British Virgin Islands, family and community are at the heart of everyday life, forming the social fabric that binds people together and shapes the identity of the territory. Strong family ties and close-knit communities are cherished values in BVI culture, with relationships and social connections playing a central role in the lives of its residents.

Families in the BVI often extend beyond the nuclear unit to include relatives, godparents, and close friends, creating a network of support and belonging that provides stability and security. Multi-generational households are common, with grandparents, parents, and children living together under one roof and sharing responsibilities for childcare, household chores, and financial support.

In addition to family bonds, community connections are also highly valued in the BVI, with neighbors, friends, and acquaintances coming together to support one another in times of need and celebrate milestones and achievements. Community events such as festivals, church gatherings, and neighborhood block parties provide opportunities for socializing, networking, and fostering a sense of belonging.

Religion plays a significant role in BVI's family and community life, with churches serving as important hubs of social and spiritual activity. Christianity is the dominant religion in the territory, with denominations such as Anglican, Methodist, Baptist, and Roman Catholicism represented in local congregations. Church services, prayer meetings, and fellowship activities offer opportunities for worship, fellowship, and community outreach, bringing people together in faith and unity.

Education is another key component of BVI's social fabric, with schools serving as important centers of learning, socialization, and community engagement. Public and private schools across the territory provide students with access to quality education, extracurricular activities, and support services that help them thrive academically, socially, and emotionally. Parent-teacher associations, school events, and volunteer opportunities encourage parental involvement and strengthen connections between schools and communities.

Community organizations and grassroots initiatives also play a vital role in BVI's social fabric, addressing a wide range of issues and concerns related to health, education, environment, and social justice. Nonprofit organizations, civic groups, and volunteer networks work tirelessly to improve the quality of life for residents, promote community development, and preserve the cultural heritage and natural resources of the territory.

As you immerse yourself in the British Virgin Islands, you'll experience firsthand the warmth, hospitality, and camaraderie of its family-oriented and community-minded culture. Whether you're sharing a meal with relatives, attending a church service, or volunteering at a local charity, you'll find that family and community are the cornerstones of BVI society, fostering connections, building relationships, and creating a sense of belonging that transcends boundaries and unites people in common purpose and shared values.

Religion and Spirituality: Faith in the Islands

In the British Virgin Islands, religion and spirituality are deeply woven into the cultural fabric of the islands, shaping the beliefs, values, and traditions of its people. Christianity is the predominant religion in the BVI, with a variety of denominations represented across the territory, including Anglican, Methodist, Baptist, Roman Catholic, and Pentecostal.

Churches serve as important centers of worship, community, and social activity, providing spiritual guidance, fellowship, and support to their congregations. Sunday worship services are a cornerstone of religious life in the BVI, with churchgoers gathering to sing hymns, pray, and listen to sermons delivered by clergy members.

The Anglican Church holds a prominent place in BVI's religious landscape, with historic churches such as St. Phillip's Church on Tortola and St. Mary's Church on Virgin Gorda serving as architectural and spiritual landmarks. These churches, dating back to the colonial era, are not only places of worship but also repositories of history and culture, with stained glass windows, wooden pews, and ancient artifacts that speak to centuries of faith and tradition.

Methodist and Baptist churches are also prevalent in the BVI, with congregations gathering in both traditional and modern worship spaces to praise God, study scripture, and engage in community outreach. These churches often host Bible studies, prayer groups, and youth programs that provide spiritual nourishment and support to members of all ages.

Roman Catholicism has a strong presence in the BVI, with several parishes and chapels scattered throughout the islands. Masses are celebrated in English and Spanish, reflecting the multicultural makeup of the territory, and special events such as First Communion, Confirmation, and Holy Week observances are eagerly anticipated by parishioners.

In addition to mainstream Christian denominations, the BVI is also home to smaller religious communities and faith traditions, including Pentecostalism, Jehovah's Witnesses, Seventh-day Adventism, and Rastafarianism. These diverse religious groups contribute to the tapestry of faith in the islands, enriching the spiritual landscape with their beliefs, practices, and rituals.

Spirituality is not confined to formal religious institutions in the BVI but is also expressed through indigenous beliefs, superstitions, and folk practices passed down through generations. For example, obeah, a traditional Afro-Caribbean religion involving the use of herbs, charms, and rituals for healing and protection, continues to be practiced by some residents alongside their Christian faith.

As you explore the British Virgin Islands, you'll encounter a rich tapestry of religious and spiritual expression that reflects the diversity, resilience, and faith of its people. Whether you're attending a church service, participating in a religious festival, or exploring the natural beauty of the islands, you'll find that religion and spirituality are integral aspects of BVI's cultural identity, guiding its people in their journey through life and connecting them to something greater than themselves.

Education System in BVI: Nurturing Minds

The education system in the British Virgin Islands (BVI) is a cornerstone of the territory's development and progress, nurturing young minds and preparing them for success in a rapidly changing world. The Ministry of Education and Culture oversees the education system, working in partnership with schools, educators, parents, and community stakeholders to ensure quality and equity in education for all students.

Education in the BVI is compulsory for children between the ages of five and 17, with primary education covering grades one through six and secondary education covering grades seven through 12. The curriculum is based on the British model of education, with an emphasis on core subjects such as English, mathematics, science, and social studies, as well as specialized subjects including art, music, physical education, and vocational training.

Primary education in the BVI focuses on laying a strong foundation in literacy, numeracy, and critical thinking skills, with a holistic approach that nurtures students' intellectual, emotional, and social development. Teachers use a variety of instructional methods and resources to engage students and cater to diverse learning styles, fostering a love of learning and a spirit of inquiry.

Secondary education builds on the foundation laid in primary school, offering students the opportunity to pursue a broad and balanced curriculum that prepares them for further study, employment, and citizenship. At the secondary level, students have the option to pursue academic or vocational pathways, with opportunities to earn internationally recognized qualifications such as the Caribbean Secondary Education Certificate (CSEC) and the Caribbean Advanced Proficiency Examination (CAPE).

In addition to traditional classroom instruction, the BVI education system places a strong emphasis on extracurricular activities, including sports, arts, and community service. Schools offer a wide range of clubs, teams, and organizations that allow students to explore their interests, develop their talents, and build leadership skills outside of the classroom.

Technology plays an increasingly important role in education in the BVI, with schools incorporating digital tools and resources into teaching and learning to enhance engagement, collaboration, and creativity. Many schools are equipped with computer labs, interactive whiteboards, and other technology infrastructure to support 21st-century learning.

The BVI government is committed to providing equal access to quality education for all students, regardless of background or ability. Efforts are underway to improve school infrastructure, enhance teacher training and professional development, and expand access to early childhood education and special needs support services.

As you delve into the education system in the British Virgin Islands, you'll discover a dynamic and evolving landscape that is dedicated to empowering students to reach their full potential, contribute to their communities, and become lifelong learners in a global society. Through collaboration, innovation, and a commitment to excellence, the BVI education system continues to nurture minds and shape futures, laying the foundation for a brighter tomorrow for all.

Healthcare and Wellness: Living Well in Paradise

Healthcare and wellness in the British Virgin Islands (BVI) are integral aspects of life in paradise, with a range of services and resources available to support residents and visitors in maintaining their physical, mental, and emotional well-being. The BVI's healthcare system is overseen by the Ministry of Health and Social Development, which works in collaboration with public and private healthcare providers to deliver high-quality medical care to the community.

The main healthcare facility in the BVI is the Peebles Hospital, located on the main island of Tortola. Peebles Hospital is a full-service hospital equipped with modern facilities and medical equipment, including emergency services, surgical suites, diagnostic imaging, and specialist clinics. The hospital provides a wide range of medical services, including primary care, maternity care, pediatrics, internal medicine, surgery, and rehabilitation.

In addition to Peebles Hospital, the BVI has several smaller clinics and health centers located throughout the islands, providing primary and preventive care services to residents in rural and remote areas. These clinics offer services such as general medical consultations, vaccinations, screenings, and health education programs to promote healthy lifestyles and prevent disease.

The BVI government is committed to improving access to healthcare services for all residents, with initiatives aimed at expanding healthcare infrastructure, recruiting and retaining qualified healthcare professionals, and enhancing the quality and efficiency of care delivery. Efforts are also underway to promote health literacy and empower individuals and communities to take an active role in managing their health and wellness.

Complementing the healthcare system in the BVI is a thriving wellness industry that offers a variety of holistic and alternative therapies to promote physical, mental, and spiritual well-being. Wellness practitioners such as massage therapists, yoga instructors, nutritionists, and holistic healers provide services ranging from massage therapy and acupuncture to meditation and herbal medicine, helping individuals achieve balance, harmony, and vitality in their lives.

The BVI's natural environment also plays a central role in promoting health and wellness, with its pristine beaches, lush landscapes, and crystal-clear waters providing the perfect backdrop for outdoor recreation and relaxation.

Residents and visitors alike enjoy a wide range of activities such as swimming, snorkeling, hiking, and yoga retreats, allowing them to connect with nature and rejuvenate their body, mind, and soul.

As you embrace the healthcare and wellness opportunities in the British Virgin Islands, you'll discover a holistic approach to health that integrates medical care, preventive measures, and lifestyle choices to help you live your best life in paradise. Whether you're seeking medical treatment at Peebles Hospital, participating in a wellness retreat, or simply enjoying the natural beauty of the islands, the BVI offers a sanctuary for health and well-being that nourishes the body, soothes the spirit, and uplifts the soul.

Economy and Trade: From Sugarcane to Tourism

The economy of the British Virgin Islands (BVI) has undergone significant transformations over the centuries, evolving from a reliance on sugarcane production to a thriving tourism-based economy. Historically, sugarcane was the primary economic driver in the BVI during the colonial period, with plantations established across the islands to cultivate sugarcane for export to Europe. However, the decline of the sugar industry in the 19th century, due to factors such as hurricanes, pests, and competition from other sugar-producing regions, led to a shift in the BVI's economic focus.

In the early 20th century, the BVI began to diversify its economy, exploring new industries such as fishing, livestock farming, and boat building. These industries provided employment opportunities and contributed to the local economy, but it was the emergence of tourism in the mid-20th century that truly transformed the BVI's economic landscape.

Tourism quickly became the leading economic sector in the BVI, driven by the territory's natural beauty, pristine beaches, and warm climate. Visitors from around the world were drawn to the BVI's idyllic setting for sailing, snorkeling, diving, and beach vacations, fueling growth in the hospitality, leisure, and service industries. Today, tourism is the mainstay of the BVI's economy, generating revenue, employment, and investment opportunities across the islands.

The tourism sector in the BVI encompasses a wide range of businesses and activities, including hotels, resorts, villas, restaurants, bars, tour operators, and water sports companies. The territory's reputation as a premier yachting destination has earned it the nickname "Sailing Capital of the World," with numerous marinas, charter companies, and regattas attracting sailors and boating enthusiasts from far and wide.

In addition to tourism, financial services also play a significant role in the BVI's economy, contributing to its status as an international financial center. The BVI's favorable tax laws, political stability, and sophisticated legal system have made it a popular jurisdiction for offshore banking, company formation, and asset protection, attracting investors, corporations, and high-net-worth individuals from around the globe.

Other sectors of the BVI's economy include agriculture, manufacturing, and retail trade, although these industries have become increasingly marginalized in favor of tourism and financial services. Efforts are underway to promote sustainable economic development and diversification, with initiatives aimed at supporting small businesses, promoting entrepreneurship, and harnessing renewable energy resources to reduce dependence on imported goods and fossil fuels.

As the BVI continues to navigate the challenges and opportunities of the 21st century, its economy remains resilient and dynamic, fueled by a spirit of innovation, entrepreneurship, and resilience. From sugarcane to tourism, the BVI's economic journey reflects its ability to adapt, evolve, and thrive in an ever-changing global landscape, shaping the future of the territory and its people for generations to come.

Transportation Networks: Getting Around the Islands

Transportation networks in the British Virgin Islands (BVI) are essential for facilitating movement and connectivity between the islands, ensuring access to goods, services, and opportunities for residents and visitors alike. With a scattered archipelago consisting of over 50 islands and cays, transportation infrastructure plays a crucial role in the daily lives of BVI residents and the tourism industry that drives the economy.

The primary mode of transportation between the islands is by boat or ferry, with numerous ferry companies operating regular routes connecting the main islands of Tortola, Virgin Gorda, Jost Van Dyke, and Anegada, as well as smaller islands and cays. Ferries provide a convenient and scenic way to travel between the islands, offering passengers stunning views of the turquoise waters and lush landscapes of the BVI.

In addition to ferries, private boat charters and water taxis are also popular means of transportation in the BVI, offering flexibility and convenience for travelers looking to explore the islands at their own pace. Private boats and yachts can be rented for day trips, island-hopping adventures, or customized excursions, allowing visitors to discover hidden coves, pristine beaches, and secluded anchorages throughout the archipelago.

On land, road transportation is the primary mode of getting around the main islands of Tortola and Virgin Gorda, with a network of paved roads and highways connecting towns, villages, and tourist attractions. Rental cars, taxis, and safari buses are readily available for hire, providing options for travelers to explore the islands independently or with the assistance of a local driver.

Although public transportation options are limited in the BVI, residents rely on privately operated minibusses, known as "safaris," for commuting and traveling between towns and neighborhoods. These colorful minibusses are a common sight on the roads of Tortola, providing affordable and reliable transportation for residents who do not own a car or prefer not to drive.

Air transportation is also an important component of the BVI's transportation network, with the territory served by two airports: Terrance B. Lettsome International Airport on Beef Island, near Tortola, and Virgin Gorda Airport on Virgin Gorda. These airports provide domestic and international flights, connecting the BVI to major gateway cities in the Caribbean and beyond.

Helicopter charter services are available for travelers seeking a faster and more scenic mode of transportation between the islands, offering aerial tours, airport transfers, and custom charters for sightseeing and special occasions. Helicopters provide an efficient way to travel between the islands, with the added benefit of panoramic views of the BVI's stunning landscapes from above.

As you navigate the transportation networks of the British Virgin Islands, you'll discover a variety of options for getting around the islands, each offering its own unique perspective and experience of this tropical paradise. Whether you're sailing on a ferry, cruising in a rental car, or soaring through the skies in a helicopter, transportation in the BVI is an adventure in itself, promising unforgettable memories and endless possibilities for exploration and discovery.

Conservation Efforts: Preserving BVI's Natural Heritage

Conservation efforts in the British Virgin Islands (BVI) are paramount to safeguarding the territory's rich biodiversity, pristine ecosystems, and natural heritage for future generations. With its stunning coral reefs, mangrove forests, and diverse wildlife, the BVI is home to a wealth of natural resources that support local livelihoods, sustain marine and terrestrial ecosystems, and attract visitors from around the world.

One of the key conservation priorities in the BVI is the protection of marine environments, including coral reefs, seagrass beds, and mangrove habitats. These ecosystems provide essential services such as coastal protection, habitat for fish and other marine life, and recreational opportunities for residents and tourists. To safeguard these valuable resources, the BVI government has established a network of marine protected areas (MPAs) and designated conservation zones where fishing, anchoring, and other human activities are regulated to minimize environmental impact and promote sustainability.

The BVI's coral reefs are particularly vulnerable to threats such as climate change, pollution, overfishing, and coastal development, which can degrade coral health and reduce biodiversity. To address these challenges, the BVI government collaborates with local and international organizations to monitor reef health, implement conservation measures, and raise awareness about the importance of coral reef protection. Initiatives such as coral reef restoration projects, marine debris clean-up efforts, and educational programs for schools and communities help to engage stakeholders and promote stewardship of the marine environment.

In addition to marine conservation, the BVI is also committed to protecting its terrestrial habitats, including forests, wetlands, and coastal areas. The territory's national parks, nature reserves, and protected areas serve as important refuges for native plants and animals, preserving biodiversity and ecological integrity. Conservation efforts focus on habitat restoration, invasive species management, and sustainable land use practices to maintain healthy ecosystems and minimize habitat loss and fragmentation.

Community involvement is crucial to the success of conservation efforts in the BVI, with local residents, businesses, and organizations playing a vital role in protecting natural resources and promoting sustainable development. Volunteer groups, environmental NGOs, and government agencies work together on conservation projects and awareness campaigns, mobilizing resources and expertise to address environmental challenges and promote conservation stewardship.

Tourism also plays a role in conservation in the BVI, with eco-tourism initiatives offering visitors the opportunity to experience the territory's natural beauty while supporting conservation efforts. Sustainable tourism practices such as low-impact activities, responsible wildlife viewing, and eco-friendly accommodations help to minimize the environmental footprint of tourism and generate revenue for conservation programs.

As the BVI continues to face environmental challenges such as climate change, habitat loss, and pollution, conservation efforts remain critical to preserving the territory's natural heritage and ensuring the long-term health and sustainability of its ecosystems. Through collaboration, innovation, and a commitment to conservation stewardship, the BVI is working to protect its natural resources and promote a more resilient and sustainable future for generations to come.

Hurricane Resilience: Weathering the Storms

Hurricane resilience is a critical aspect of life in the British Virgin Islands (BVI), where the threat of tropical storms and hurricanes looms large during the Atlantic hurricane season, which typically runs from June to November each year. Situated in the hurricane belt of the Caribbean, the BVI is vulnerable to the impacts of these powerful storms, which can bring destructive winds, heavy rainfall, storm surges, and flooding.

Over the years, the BVI has experienced numerous hurricanes, including devastating storms such as Hurricane Irma in 2017, which caused widespread destruction and loss of life across the territory. In the aftermath of such disasters, the resilience of the BVI's communities is put to the test as residents come together to rebuild homes, restore infrastructure, and revitalize the economy.

Hurricane preparedness and disaster management are top priorities for the BVI government, with agencies such as the Department of Disaster Management (DDM) responsible for coordinating emergency response efforts, providing public education and outreach, and developing disaster risk reduction strategies.

The DDM works closely with local authorities, international partners, and non-governmental organizations to ensure a coordinated and effective response to hurricanes and other natural disasters.

One key aspect of hurricane resilience in the BVI is building codes and regulations designed to enhance the structural integrity of buildings and infrastructure and minimize damage from high winds and storm surge. New construction projects must adhere to strict building standards, including the use of hurricane-resistant materials, reinforced foundations, and wind-resistant roofing systems, to withstand the force of a hurricane.

In addition to infrastructure improvements, the BVI invests in early warning systems, meteorological monitoring, and emergency communication networks to provide timely and accurate information to residents and visitors in the event of a hurricane. The National Emergency Operations Center (NEOC) serves as the nerve center for disaster response and coordination, facilitating communication between government agencies, emergency services, and the public during emergencies.

Community resilience is also a vital component of hurricane preparedness in the BVI, with initiatives such as community emergency response teams (CERTs), neighborhood watch programs, and disaster preparedness training workshops helping to empower residents to take proactive measures to protect themselves, their families, and their property during hurricanes.

Despite the challenges posed by hurricanes, the BVI's resilience and spirit of resilience shine through in the face of adversity, with communities coming together to support one another, rebuild stronger, and emerge stronger than before. Through preparedness, planning, and cooperation, the BVI continues to weather the storms and remain resilient in the face of nature's fury, ensuring the safety and well-being of its residents and the sustainability of its communities for generations to come.

British Influence: Legacy and Impact

The British influence on the British Virgin Islands (BVI) is deeply rooted in the territory's history, culture, and governance, shaping its identity and development in significant ways. As a British Overseas Territory, the BVI has been under British sovereignty since the 17th century, when the islands were first settled by European colonists.

One of the most enduring legacies of British influence in the BVI is its legal system, which is based on English common law and reflects the principles of justice, fairness, and due process. The BVI's legal framework encompasses statutes, case law, and legal precedents inherited from the British legal system, providing a solid foundation for the territory's judicial system and legal institutions.

Another aspect of British influence in the BVI is its political structure and governance model, which is based on the British parliamentary system and features a Governor appointed by the British monarch as the head of state, a local legislature known as the House of Assembly, and a Cabinet of Ministers responsible for executive functions. The BVI's political institutions and administrative practices reflect

British traditions of democracy, rule of law, and accountability, while also incorporating elements of local autonomy and self-government.

The British influence on the BVI extends beyond its legal and political systems to its cultural heritage, language, and education. English is the official language of the BVI, spoken by the majority of the population and used in government, education, business, and everyday communication. British cultural traditions, such as afternoon tea, cricket, and the celebration of British holidays like Queen's Birthday, are also observed in the BVI, reflecting the territory's ties to its colonial past.

Education in the BVI is heavily influenced by the British educational system, with schools following a curriculum based on British standards and offering internationally recognized qualifications such as the Caribbean Secondary Education Certificate (CSEC) and the Caribbean Advanced Proficiency Examination (CAPE). Many BVI students pursue higher education in the United Kingdom or other Commonwealth countries, further deepening their ties to British culture and society.

In addition to its legal, political, cultural, and educational influences, the British legacy in the BVI is also evident in its infrastructure, architecture, and social institutions. British colonial architecture can be seen in historic buildings and landmarks throughout the territory, while British names and place names are common in towns, streets, and geographical features.

Overall, the British influence has left a lasting impact on the British Virgin Islands, shaping its identity, institutions, and way of life. While the BVI has evolved and diversified over the centuries, its ties to Britain remain strong, providing a sense of continuity, stability, and connection to its colonial past.

American Connection: Shared Histories and Futures

The American connection to the British Virgin Islands (BVI) is a significant aspect of the territory's history, culture, and economy. Situated just east of the United States Virgin Islands (USVI) and within close proximity to Puerto Rico, the BVI has long-standing ties to the United States, shaped by shared histories, cultural exchanges, and economic interactions.

One of the earliest connections between the BVI and the United States dates back to the colonial era when the islands served as a strategic outpost for British naval forces and American privateers during the Revolutionary War. The BVI's geographic location made it a focal point for trade, smuggling, and maritime activities between the American colonies and the Caribbean, contributing to the territory's economic prosperity and strategic importance.

During the 20th century, the American connection to the BVI deepened with the growth of tourism and investment from the United States. American travelers began visiting the BVI in increasing numbers, drawn to its pristine beaches, crystal-clear waters, and laid-back island vibe. The development of tourism infrastructure, including hotels, resorts, and marinas, catered to American tourists, fueling growth in the hospitality and service industries and creating employment opportunities for locals.

In addition to tourism, the BVI's economy has benefited from American investment and business interests, with many American companies establishing operations in the territory. The BVI's status as a premier offshore financial center has attracted American investors, corporations, and individuals seeking tax advantages, asset protection, and financial services such as company formation, banking, and trust management.

Culturally, the American connection is evident in the BVI's music, cuisine, and popular culture, which have been influenced by American trends, tastes, and traditions. American music genres such as jazz, blues, and rock 'n' roll are popular in the BVI, with local musicians incorporating these influences into their own musical styles. American cuisine, including hamburgers, hot dogs, and barbecue, is also enjoyed by locals and visitors alike, alongside traditional Caribbean dishes.

The future of the American connection to the BVI holds opportunities for continued collaboration and partnership in areas such as tourism, trade, and sustainable development. As the BVI seeks to diversify its economy, attract investment, and promote sustainable growth, its relationship with the United States will remain integral to its success and prosperity.

Overall, the American connection to the BVI is a dynamic and multifaceted relationship that reflects the shared histories, interests, and aspirations of both territories. From colonial ties to modern-day partnerships, the bond between the BVI and the United States continues to shape the destiny of the islands and the people who call them home.

Caribbean Identity: BVI's Place in the Region

The British Virgin Islands (BVI) hold a unique position within the broader Caribbean region, characterized by a rich tapestry of cultural, historical, and geographical influences that shape its identity and place in the world. Situated in the northeastern Caribbean, the BVI is part of the Lesser Antilles archipelago, surrounded by the turquoise waters of the Caribbean Sea and the Atlantic Ocean.

As a territory with a diverse population representing various ethnicities, nationalities, and cultural backgrounds, the BVI embodies the spirit of the Caribbean, a region renowned for its vibrant culture, warm hospitality, and breathtaking natural beauty. Despite its small size, the BVI's influence extends far beyond its shores, serving as a gateway to the wider Caribbean and a melting pot of Caribbean, European, African, and American influences.

Historically, the BVI's identity has been shaped by waves of migration, colonization, and cultural exchange, beginning with the indigenous Arawak and Carib peoples who inhabited the islands prior to European contact. The arrival of European colonists, including the Spanish, Dutch, and British, brought new languages, religions, and customs to the BVI, leaving a lasting imprint on its cultural landscape.

The BVI's Caribbean identity is reflected in its music, cuisine, festivals, and traditions, which draw inspiration from African, European, and indigenous cultures. Calypso, reggae, soca, and steelpan music are popular in the BVI, reflecting the region's diverse musical heritage and rhythms. Caribbean cuisine, characterized by fresh seafood, tropical fruits, and spices, is enjoyed by locals and visitors alike, with dishes such as conch fritters, jerk chicken, and roti showcasing the culinary diversity of the region.

Festivals and celebrations are an integral part of Caribbean life, and the BVI is no exception, with events such as the Emancipation Festival, the BVI Spring Regatta, and the Virgin Gorda Easter Festival attracting crowds from near and far. These celebrations offer an opportunity for residents to come together, celebrate their shared heritage, and showcase the unique cultural traditions of the islands.

Geographically, the BVI's location at the crossroads of the Caribbean makes it an ideal destination for travelers seeking sun, sea, and sand, with its pristine beaches, secluded coves, and lush landscapes attracting visitors from around the world. The BVI's reputation as a premier sailing destination, coupled with its rich maritime history and vibrant marine life, further enhances its allure as a Caribbean paradise.

Despite its small size, the BVI punches above its weight on the global stage, serving as a center for international finance, tourism, and commerce in the Caribbean. Its status as a British Overseas Territory affords it political stability, economic security, and access to global markets, while its natural beauty and warm climate make it a magnet for investors, entrepreneurs, and adventurers alike.

In summary, the British Virgin Islands' Caribbean identity is a reflection of its rich cultural heritage, geographical location, and historical ties to the region. As a microcosm of the Caribbean, the BVI embodies the diversity, resilience, and vibrancy that define the spirit of the Caribbean, serving as a beacon of hope, inspiration, and opportunity for all who call it home.

Local Dialects and Languages: Communicating in BVI

In the British Virgin Islands (BVI), communication is a colorful tapestry woven from various local dialects and languages that reflect the territory's diverse cultural heritage and history. While English is the official language of the BVI and widely spoken by the majority of the population, there are also local dialects and creole languages that add richness and depth to everyday conversations.

One of the most distinctive features of BVI's language landscape is the use of Virgin Islands Creole English (VCE), also known as Virgin Islands English Creole or simply "dialect" by locals. VCE is a unique blend of English, African, and West Indian influences, characterized by its rhythmic cadence, colorful expressions, and distinctive vocabulary. It is spoken by many residents in informal settings and is an integral part of BVI's cultural identity.

In addition to VCE, the BVI is home to other local dialects and variations of English spoken by different communities across the islands. These dialects may vary in pronunciation, vocabulary, and grammar, reflecting the diverse origins and backgrounds of the BVI's population. While some dialects may be more prevalent in certain areas or among specific demographic groups, they all contribute to the rich linguistic tapestry of the territory.

Despite the presence of local dialects, standard English is the language of instruction in schools, used in government, business, and official communications, and widely understood by residents and visitors alike. BVI's education system emphasizes proficiency in English, with students taught to read, write, and communicate effectively in the language from an early age.

In addition to English and local dialects, other languages are also spoken in the BVI, reflecting the territory's multicultural makeup and international connections. Spanish, for example, is spoken by a significant number of residents, particularly those with ties to Spanish-speaking countries in the Caribbean and Latin America. Other languages, such as French, Dutch, and Portuguese, may also be spoken by expatriates, tourists, and members of the international community.

Overall, the language landscape of the BVI is a reflection of its cultural diversity, history, and global connections. Whether speaking standard English, local dialects, or other languages, communication in the BVI is a vibrant and dynamic process that bridges differences, fosters understanding, and celebrates the unique identity of the territory and its people.

Cultural Etiquette: Navigating Social Norms

Navigating cultural etiquette in the British Virgin Islands (BVI) requires an understanding of the social norms, customs, and traditions that shape interactions and relationships among residents and visitors. While the BVI is known for its laid-back and friendly atmosphere, there are certain cultural practices and etiquette guidelines that are important to observe to show respect and appreciation for local customs.

One aspect of cultural etiquette in the BVI is the importance of greeting others with warmth and friendliness. Handshakes are common when meeting someone for the first time, followed by a polite exchange of pleasantries. It is also customary to address people by their title and last name, such as "Mr. Smith" or "Ms. Jones," until given permission to use their first name.

Respect for elders and authority figures is another key aspect of cultural etiquette in the BVI. It is customary to greet elders with deference and to show courtesy and respect in interactions with individuals in positions of authority, such as government officials, community leaders, and elders within the community.

Hospitality is highly valued in BVI culture, and guests are often welcomed with open arms and treated with generosity and kindness. It is considered polite to accept offers of food, drink, or hospitality graciously and to express gratitude for the hospitality extended to you.

In social settings, punctuality is appreciated but not always strictly adhered to, as island time tends to be more relaxed and flexible. It is considered polite to arrive within a reasonable timeframe of the agreed-upon meeting time but to be understanding if others are running late.

When dining in the BVI, it is customary to wait for the host or hostess to invite you to begin eating before starting your meal. Table manners are generally informal, but it is important to eat with your mouth closed, avoid speaking with food in your mouth, and use utensils rather than fingers when appropriate.

Dress codes vary depending on the occasion and location, but casual attire is generally acceptable for most social gatherings and events in the BVI. However, more formal attire may be required for certain occasions, such as weddings, religious ceremonies, or business meetings.

Respecting local customs and traditions, such as participating in cultural festivals and celebrations, is also an important aspect of cultural etiquette in the BVI. By embracing and appreciating the rich cultural heritage of the islands, visitors can forge deeper connections with the local community and gain a greater understanding of BVI culture.

Overall, cultural etiquette in the BVI is about showing respect, kindness, and consideration for others, while also embracing the unique customs and traditions of the islands. By observing these cultural norms and practices, visitors can navigate social interactions with grace and sensitivity, fostering meaningful connections and experiences during their time in the British Virgin Islands.

Traditional Dress and Attire: Fashion in the Islands

Fashion in the British Virgin Islands (BVI) is a reflection of the territory's rich cultural heritage, climate, and lifestyle. While modern Western attire is common in everyday life, traditional dress and attire still hold significance in certain cultural events, festivals, and ceremonies, providing a glimpse into the islands' history and traditions.

One example of traditional dress in the BVI is the Madras fabric, a brightly colored cotton fabric with intricate patterns and designs that originated in India and was brought to the Caribbean by colonial traders. Madras fabric is commonly used to make dresses, skirts, shirts, and headwraps worn by both men and women during special occasions such as weddings, festivals, and cultural celebrations.

Another traditional garment worn in the BVI is the quadrille dress, a full-skirted dress made from lightweight fabric such as cotton or linen, typically worn by women during quadrille dances, a popular folk dance tradition in the Caribbean. Quadrille dresses are often brightly colored and adorned with ruffles, lace, and other decorative elements, reflecting the festive spirit of the dance.

For men, traditional attire in the BVI may include the sloop-sailed pants, also known as "sloop johnnies," which are loose-fitting pants made from lightweight fabric and worn with a matching shirt or vest. Sloop-sailed pants are commonly worn during cultural events, regattas, and other maritime celebrations in the BVI, reflecting the territory's seafaring heritage. In addition to traditional dress, contemporary fashion in the BVI is influenced by the tropical climate and outdoor lifestyle, with lightweight, breathable fabrics such as cotton, linen, and rayon being popular choices for everyday attire. Casual clothing such as shorts, t-shirts, sundresses, and sandals are commonly worn by both locals and visitors, reflecting the relaxed and laid-back atmosphere of island life.

For more formal occasions, such as weddings, religious ceremonies, or business meetings, men may opt for suits or dress shirts paired with trousers, while women may choose dresses or skirts paired with blouses or tops. Light colors and natural fabrics are preferred to stay cool in the tropical heat, while accessories such as hats, sunglasses, and scarves add a touch of style and flair to outfits.

Overall, fashion in the BVI is a blend of traditional and contemporary styles, reflecting the territory's cultural diversity, climate, and lifestyle. Whether dressing for a cultural event, a day at the beach, or a night out on the town, residents and visitors alike embrace the colorful and vibrant fashion of the islands, creating a unique and dynamic sartorial landscape in the British Virgin Islands.

Sports and Recreation: Active Lifestyles in BVI

Sports and recreation play an integral role in the lifestyle of the British Virgin Islands (BVI), offering residents and visitors alike a myriad of opportunities to stay active, explore the natural beauty of the islands, and engage in friendly competition. With its stunning landscapes, pristine beaches, and crystal-clear waters, the BVI provides the perfect backdrop for a wide range of outdoor activities and sporting pursuits.

One of the most popular sports in the BVI is sailing, thanks to its rich maritime heritage, favorable trade winds, and sheltered anchorages. The territory hosts numerous sailing regattas and races throughout the year, including the world-renowned BVI Spring Regatta and Sailing Festival, which attract sailors from around the globe to compete in a series of thrilling races and festivities.

In addition to sailing, water sports such as snorkeling, diving, kayaking, and paddleboarding are also immensely popular in the BVI, allowing enthusiasts to explore the vibrant marine life, coral reefs, and hidden coves that dot the coastline. With warm waters year-round and excellent visibility, the BVI is a paradise for water sports enthusiasts of all skill levels. For those who prefer activities on land, hiking and trekking offer a unique opportunity to discover the BVI's diverse landscapes, from lush rainforests and scenic trails to rugged mountain peaks and panoramic vistas. Popular hiking destinations include Sage Mountain National Park, Gorda Peak National Park, and the trails of Virgin Gorda's Baths, each offering breathtaking views and opportunities for adventure. Other outdoor activities in the BVI include beach volleyball, tennis, golf, and horseback riding, providing options for individuals and families to enjoy active pursuits in the sunshine. Local sports clubs and organizations also offer opportunities for organized sports leagues, fitness classes, and recreational activities, fostering a sense of community and camaraderie among participants.

In addition to traditional sports and recreation, the BVI's cultural events and festivals often incorporate athletic competitions and games, such as tug-of-war, sack races, and greased pole climbing, adding an element of fun and excitement to celebrations throughout the year.

Overall, sports and recreation in the BVI cater to a wide range of interests and abilities, encouraging people to stay active, connect with nature, and embrace the outdoor lifestyle that defines the spirit of the islands. Whether sailing the azure waters, hiking the scenic trails, or participating in a friendly game of beach volleyball, the BVI offers endless opportunities for adventure, exploration, and enjoyment in the great outdoors.

Environmental Sustainability: Green Initiatives

Environmental sustainability is a key focus in the British Virgin Islands (BVI), where efforts are underway to preserve the natural beauty and ecological integrity of the islands for future generations. As a region known for its stunning landscapes, rich biodiversity, and fragile ecosystems, the BVI recognizes the importance of adopting green initiatives to mitigate the impacts of climate change, conserve natural resources, and promote sustainable development.

One of the primary areas of focus in environmental sustainability in the BVI is the conservation of marine and coastal ecosystems. The territory is home to extensive coral reefs, mangrove forests, and seagrass beds that provide critical habitats for a diverse array of marine life, including fish, turtles, and corals. To protect these valuable ecosystems, the BVI has implemented marine protected areas, such as the Virgin Islands National Park and the Jost Van Dyke Preservation Society, which aim to safeguard vulnerable marine habitats and promote sustainable fishing practices.

In addition to marine conservation, the BVI is also committed to reducing its carbon footprint and promoting renewable energy sources. Solar energy, in particular, has gained traction in recent years, with numerous solar power projects and initiatives underway to harness the abundant sunshine and reduce dependence on fossil fuels. The BVI's government has also introduced incentives and policies to encourage the adoption of energy-efficient technologies and practices, such as LED lighting, energy-efficient appliances, and building design standards that prioritize sustainability and energy conservation.

Land conservation is another important aspect of environmental sustainability in the BVI, with efforts focused on preserving natural habitats, protecting biodiversity, and promoting responsible land use practices. The BVI National Parks Trust manages a network of protected areas and nature reserves, encompassing diverse ecosystems ranging from tropical rainforests and dry forests to coastal wetlands and volcanic landscapes. These protected areas serve as important refuges for native flora and fauna, as well as popular destinations for eco-tourism and outdoor recreation.

Water conservation is also a priority in the BVI, given the territory's reliance on rainwater harvesting and limited freshwater resources. Public awareness campaigns and educational programs promote water-saving practices, such as using water-efficient fixtures, repairing leaks, and practicing responsible water management in households and businesses.

Overall, environmental sustainability in the BVI is a multifaceted endeavor that involves government action, community engagement, and individual responsibility. By implementing green initiatives, conserving natural resources, and embracing sustainable practices, the BVI aims to safeguard its environment, promote resilience to climate change, and ensure a bright and sustainable future for generations to come.

Legal System and Justice: Laws of the Land

The legal system and justice in the British Virgin Islands (BVI) are governed by a combination of British common law, local statutes, and customary practices that reflect the territory's colonial history and cultural heritage. As a British Overseas Territory, the BVI operates under a legal framework that is based on English law, with adaptations to suit the unique needs and circumstances of the territory.

The highest court in the BVI is the Eastern Caribbean Supreme Court, which is divided into two divisions: the High Court and the Court of Appeal. The High Court has jurisdiction over civil and criminal matters, while the Court of Appeal hears appeals from decisions made by the High Court and other lower courts in the Eastern Caribbean.

In addition to the Eastern Caribbean Supreme Court, the BVI has its own local court system, which includes the Magistrates' Court and the Juvenile Court. These courts handle a wide range of cases, including minor criminal offenses, civil disputes, family matters, and juvenile delinquency.

The legal profession in the BVI is regulated by the Virgin Islands Bar Association, which sets standards for admission to the bar, ethical conduct, and professional development for attorneys practicing in the territory. Lawyers in the BVI are required to adhere to strict ethical guidelines and professional standards to ensure the integrity and fairness of the legal system.

One unique feature of the legal system in the BVI is the existence of the Financial Services Division of the High Court, which handles matters related to the territory's thriving offshore financial services industry. This specialized court has jurisdiction over disputes involving international business companies, trusts, banking, and other financial matters, reflecting the importance of the financial services sector to the BVI's economy.

The BVI also has its own body of legislation, known as statutes, which cover a wide range of legal areas, including corporate law, immigration, land tenure, and environmental protection. These statutes are enacted by the local legislature, known as the House of Assembly, and play a crucial role in shaping the legal landscape of the territory.

In addition to formal legal mechanisms, the BVI also has a system of customary law and community-based dispute resolution mechanisms that are rooted in the territory's cultural traditions and history. These informal systems of justice often involve mediation, arbitration, and consensus-building processes to resolve conflicts and disputes within the community.

Overall, the legal system and justice in the BVI are characterized by a blend of British legal traditions, local statutes, and customary practices that reflect the unique cultural, historical, and economic context of the territory. By upholding the rule of law, protecting individual rights, and ensuring access to justice for all residents, the BVI strives to maintain a fair, transparent, and effective legal system that serves the needs of its people and contributes to the territory's continued growth and development.

Tourism Industry: Driving Force of the Economy

The tourism industry serves as the backbone of the economy in the British Virgin Islands (BVI), playing a pivotal role in driving economic growth, generating employment opportunities, and stimulating local businesses. With its breathtaking natural beauty, pristine beaches, and vibrant culture, the BVI attracts visitors from around the world who come to explore its scenic landscapes, indulge in water sports, and immerse themselves in the laid-back island lifestyle.

Catering to a diverse range of interests and preferences, the BVI offers an array of attractions and activities for tourists to enjoy. From sailing and snorkeling to hiking and beachcombing, the territory boasts an abundance of outdoor adventures and recreational opportunities that appeal to nature lovers, adventure seekers, and sun-seekers alike.

One of the main draws for tourists in the BVI is its reputation as a premier sailing destination. The territory's sheltered anchorages, steady trade winds, and picturesque islands make it an ideal playground for sailors, yachtsmen, and boating enthusiasts. The annual BVI Spring Regatta and Sailing Festival, along with other sailing events throughout the year, attract participants and spectators from around the globe, contributing to the vibrant maritime culture of the islands.

In addition to sailing, the BVI is renowned for its world-class diving and snorkeling sites, which showcase vibrant coral reefs, colorful marine life, and underwater wrecks. Popular dive sites such as the Wreck of the Rhone, The Indians, and The Baths offer unforgettable experiences for underwater enthusiasts, while snorkeling spots like Norman Island's Caves and Sandy Spit's coral gardens provide opportunities for up-close encounters with tropical fish and sea turtles.

Land-based activities also abound in the BVI, with opportunities for hiking, birdwatching, and exploring the islands' natural wonders. Sage Mountain National Park, Virgin Gorda's Baths, and Anegada's salt ponds are just a few examples of the diverse landscapes and ecosystems that await visitors eager to discover the beauty of the islands.

The tourism industry in the BVI is not only a source of leisure and recreation but also a significant contributor to the local economy. Tourist spending on accommodations, dining, transportation, and activities generates revenue for hotels, restaurants, tour operators, and other businesses, supporting jobs and livelihoods across various sectors.

To support and sustain the tourism industry, the BVI government invests in infrastructure development, marketing initiatives, and environmental conservation efforts to ensure the long-term viability and success of the sector. Initiatives such as the BVI Tourist Board's promotional campaigns, eco-tourism projects, and sustainable tourism practices help to preserve the natural beauty and cultural heritage of the islands while enhancing the visitor experience.

Overall, tourism remains a driving force of the economy in the British Virgin Islands, contributing to economic prosperity, cultural exchange, and environmental stewardship. By welcoming visitors with warm hospitality and offering memorable experiences that showcase the best of what the islands have to offer, the BVI continues to thrive as a premier destination in the Caribbean and a paradise for travelers seeking adventure, relaxation, and authentic island experiences.

Historical Landmarks and Heritage Sites

Exploring the historical landmarks and heritage sites of the British Virgin Islands (BVI) is like embarking on a journey through time, where each site tells a story of the territory's rich and diverse history. From ancient Amerindian settlements to colonial-era forts and sugar plantations, the BVI is home to a treasure trove of cultural heritage that reflects its unique blend of indigenous, African, European, and Caribbean influences.

One of the most iconic landmarks in the BVI is the Copper Mine National Park on Virgin Gorda, which preserves the remnants of a 19th-century copper mining operation that dates back to the days of British colonial rule. Visitors to the park can explore the ruins of mine shafts, smelting furnaces, and other structures that offer a glimpse into the island's industrial past.

Another must-visit historical site is the Virgin Islands Folk Museum in Road Town, Tortola, which showcases artifacts, photographs, and exhibits that illustrate the cultural heritage and traditions of the BVI. From traditional crafts and folk art to historical documents and archaeological finds, the museum provides valuable insights into the territory's social, economic, and cultural history.

For those interested in the colonial history of the BVI, the territory boasts several well-preserved forts and historic sites that offer a glimpse into its strategic importance during the era of European expansion and empire-building. Examples include Fort Burt, Fort Charlotte, and Fort Recovery, which were built by the British to defend against pirate attacks and rival colonial powers.

The ruins of sugar plantations scattered throughout the islands are also poignant reminders of the BVI's past as a major producer of sugar cane and rum during the plantation era. Estate houses, windmills, and slave quarters can still be found on islands such as Tortola, Virgin Gorda, and Jost Van Dyke, serving as tangible links to the territory's agricultural heritage and the legacy of slavery.

In addition to these landmarks, the BVI is home to several historic churches, such as St. Phillip's Anglican Church in Road Town and the Church of the Blessed Virgin Mary in Virgin Gorda, which showcase architectural styles ranging from Georgian and Gothic to Caribbean vernacular.

Exploring these historical landmarks and heritage sites offers visitors a deeper understanding of the BVI's past and its significance in shaping the cultural identity of the territory. Whether marveling at ancient petroglyphs, touring colonial forts, or wandering through sugar mill ruins, each site provides a window into the rich tapestry of history that makes the British Virgin Islands a truly fascinating destination for travelers seeking to explore the past while enjoying the beauty of the present.

Indigenous People: Guardians of BVI's Past

The indigenous people of the British Virgin Islands (BVI) have a rich and storied history that stretches back thousands of years. Long before the arrival of European settlers, the islands were inhabited by Amerindian peoples, including the Arawak and Carib tribes, who lived off the land and sea, practicing fishing, hunting, and agriculture.

These indigenous peoples were skilled navigators and seafarers, traveling between the islands in dugout canoes and trading goods such as pottery, shells, and foodstuffs. They established villages along the coastlines, where they built homes, cultivated crops, and developed social and religious customs that were closely tied to their natural surroundings.

Evidence of their presence can still be found throughout the BVI in the form of archaeological sites, shell middens, and petroglyphs, which offer valuable insights into their way of life and cultural practices. Sites such as the Cinnamon Bay Archaeological Site on St. John in the nearby U.S. Virgin Islands provide evidence of Amerindian settlements dating back over a thousand years, including artifacts such as pottery, tools, and ceremonial objects.

The arrival of European explorers and colonists in the 15th and 16th centuries brought significant changes to the lives of the indigenous peoples of the BVI. Contact with European diseases, warfare, and forced labor led to the decline of indigenous populations, while the introduction of European goods and technology transformed traditional lifestyles and economies.

Despite these challenges, traces of indigenous culture and heritage persist in the BVI today, with place names, linguistic influences, and cultural traditions that reflect the enduring legacy of the islands' first inhabitants. Efforts to preserve and celebrate indigenous heritage are ongoing, with initiatives such as archaeological research, cultural education programs, and the establishment of heritage sites and interpretive centers that aim to honor the contributions of the indigenous peoples to the history and identity of the BVI.

In recent years, there has been a growing recognition of the importance of indigenous knowledge and perspectives in efforts to address contemporary challenges such as environmental conservation, sustainable development, and cultural revitalization. By acknowledging the legacy of the indigenous peoples and integrating their wisdom and values into modern society, the BVI seeks to honor their memory and ensure that their contributions are remembered and respected for generations to come.

Future Prospects: Vision for a Thriving BVI

The future prospects of the British Virgin Islands (BVI) are filled with promise and potential as the territory strives to build upon its strengths and address the challenges of the 21st century. With its stunning natural beauty, vibrant culture, and strategic location in the Caribbean, the BVI is well-positioned to capitalize on opportunities for economic growth, social development, and environmental sustainability.

One of the key areas of focus for the future of the BVI is economic diversification. While the tourism industry remains a vital driver of the economy, efforts are underway to expand into new sectors such as financial services, renewable energy, and information technology. By leveraging its reputation as an international financial center and fostering innovation and entrepreneurship, the BVI aims to attract investment, create jobs, and stimulate economic growth in a sustainable and inclusive manner. In addition to economic diversification, the BVI is committed to promoting environmental conservation and sustainability. As a small island territory vulnerable to the impacts of climate change and environmental degradation, the BVI recognizes the importance of protecting its natural resources, reducing carbon emissions, and adapting to changing environmental conditions. Initiatives such as the BVI National Parks Trust, the Green Energy Program, and sustainable tourism practices demonstrate the territory's commitment to preserving its pristine landscapes and promoting eco-friendly development. Social development and education are also priorities for the future of the BVI. By investing in education, healthcare, and social services, the territory aims to improve the quality of life for its residents and empower future generations to succeed in a rapidly changing world. Initiatives such as the BVI Scholarship Program, vocational training programs, and community development projects seek to enhance opportunities for learning, skill-building, and personal growth, thereby strengthening the social fabric of the territory and fostering a sense of pride and belonging among its people. Furthermore, the BVI recognizes the importance of good governance, transparency, and accountability in shaping its future trajectory. By upholding the rule of law, promoting democratic principles, and fostering a culture of integrity and ethics, the territory aims to build trust and confidence among its citizens and stakeholders, thereby laying the foundation for sustainable development and prosperity.

Overall, the vision for a thriving BVI is one of resilience, innovation, and inclusivity. By embracing opportunities for economic diversification, environmental sustainability, social development, and good governance, the territory aspires to create a brighter and more prosperous future for all who call the BVI home.

Epilogue

In reflecting on the journey through the British Virgin Islands (BVI), one can't help but marvel at the tapestry of experiences, histories, and cultures woven together in this captivating archipelago. From the lush green hills to the turquoise waters, the BVI is a place of natural wonder and human resilience, where the past and present intersect in a vibrant mosaic of island life.

As we come to the end of this exploration, it's worth pausing to consider the enduring legacy of the BVI and its significance in the wider context of the Caribbean and the world. From its indigenous roots to its colonial past and modern aspirations, the BVI embodies the complexities and contradictions of history, where triumphs and tragedies coexist amidst the beauty of the landscape.

Looking ahead, the future of the BVI holds both challenges and opportunities. Climate change, economic uncertainty, and social inequality are just a few of the issues facing the territory as it navigates the complexities of the 21st century. Yet, amidst these challenges, there is also hope and resilience, as the people of the BVI come together to chart a course towards a brighter tomorrow.

In the epilogue of our journey, let us remember the lessons learned and the stories shared, as we bid farewell to the British Virgin Islands with a sense of gratitude and wonder. For in the end, it is the people and places that we encounter along the way that leave the deepest impressions on our hearts and minds, reminding us of the beauty and resilience of the human spirit in the face of adversity.

As we close this chapter and turn the final page, may we carry with us the memories and moments that have shaped our understanding of the BVI and its place in the world. And may we always hold in our hearts the spirit of adventure and discovery that has guided us on this journey through the islands of the British Virgin Islands.

Printed in Dunstable, United Kingdom